A NECESSAR

CW00520666

Written and devised by

Deborah Clair & Philippa Urquhart

Deborah.
Clair

Philippa Urquhart

First published in paperback in Great Britain by Methuen 2018

1 3 5 7 9 10 8 6 4 2

Methuen
Orchard House
Railway Street
Slingsby, York, YO62 4AN

Methuen Publishing Limited Reg. No. 3543167

www.methuen.co.uk

A CIP catalogue record for this title is available from the British Library

ISBN: 978–0–413–77823–9

Typeset by SX Composing DTP, Rayleigh, Essex
Printed and bound in Great Britain by
CPI Group (UK) Ltd, Croydon, CR0 4YY

*Dedicated to Emily Wilding Davison
and all the unsung heroines
in Parliament and everywhere . . .*

A Necessary Woman

A Necessary Woman was first presented by CLAIR/OBSCUR in the Caryl Churchill Theatre at Royal Holloway, University of London on 7th March 2018.

The play was presented in the Macmillan Room, Portcullis House at the Houses of Parliament on 26th March 2018 to commemorate the centenary of the Representation of the People Act and as a tribute to Emily Wilding Davison, who made the ultimate sacrifice for the Cause at the Epsom Derby two years later.

A Necessary Woman was also performed in the Davison family home of Morpeth on 11th September 2018 on the eve of the unveiling of a new statue of Emily Davison in Carlisle Park.

On all three occasions the play was performed with the following cast and production team:

Emily Davison	Deborah Clair
Mary Tatton	Philippa Urquhart
Directed by	Dominique Gerrard
Sound Design by	Rich Keeble
Costumes by	Georgie Lancaster
Wigs by	Lorraine Collett
Set by	Mick Webb

The March of the Women was written by Cicely Hamilton (1872–1952) and composed by Dame Ethel Smyth (1858–1944). In our production the singer was Jane Kirby.

CLAIR/OBSCUR is a theatre company founded by Deborah Clair to shed new light on classic stories from authors or famous figures. The company derives its name from the term *chiaroscuro*, a strong, self-conscious juxtaposition of light and shade.

Authors' Note

A Necessary Woman is a re-imagining of suffragette Emily Davison's protest by hiding in a cleaning cupboard in St Mary's Undercroft in Parliament on Census Night 1911. Emily's residence was recorded as the House of Commons by P. E. Ridge, the Clerk of Works, Houses of Parliament when she was discovered on Monday 3rd April. The play is based on factual evidence gathered from Parliamentary Archives.

As actors working on our script, we found the best staging solution to adequately depict the cleaning cupboard, which did not interfere with audience sightlines, was to mark the cupboard area with three wooden crates and to construct a solid door frame with an imaginary door. The opening and closing of the door is always mimed so all action and reactions are clearly seen by the audience.

During our research for this play two significant discoveries were made. The first was that Emily intended to hide in the House of Commons and to make a speech during Prime Minister's Questions. Emily's final speech in *A Necessary Woman* was developed from the actual speech she intended to make in Parliament on Monday 3rd April 1911.

The second was a discovery made by Deborah Clair of previously unidentified film footage of Emily Davison on a march in June 1910 in the BFI film archives. Until this discovery the only known film footage of the suffragette was of her fatal actions at the Epsom Derby on 4th June 1913.

Deborah Clair and Philippa Urquhart

A Note about Emily's speech

In her original speech Emily referred to 'women of England.' There is, however, freedom to change 'England' to 'Great Britain' or 'Britain' as was done when the play was performed at the Edinburgh Festival Fringe in 2018 (see pages 24, 40 and 41 below).

Characters

Emily Davison   a member of the Women's Social and Political Union

Mary Tatton   a maid in Speaker Lowther's household

Scene One

St Mary's Chapel Undercroft, Palace of Westminster, Friday 31st March 1911, a quarter to five in the afternoon.

[House lights down to black

Sounds of protest, shouting, a window being smashed. The final guided tour of the day can be heard being ushered up the undercroft stairs. The lights go out and there is the sound of a key turning in a lock.

Enter **Emily**

*[She emerges into the half-light from the shadows, creeps across to the cupboard, mimes opening the door, takes her hat off and enters the cupboard. There are three crates, a tin bucket and a polish box in the cupboard. **Emily** barricades the door with boxes. She unbuttons her coat, removes her feather boa and tucks this and her gloves away. Opening her bag she removes a lamp and places it on the floor. Taking out matches, she lights the lamp and then raises it into view and places it on a crate. **Emily** settles herself and begins to pray.]*

Emily Saint Joan of Arc, patron of France, my patron saint, I ask you now to fight this battle with me by prayer, just as you led your troops to victory in battle. You, who were filled with the Holy Spirit and chosen by God, help me this day with the favour I ask. Grant me by your divine and powerful intercession, the courage and strength I need to endure this constant fight. Oh St. Joan, help me to be victorious in the tasks God presents to me.

[*Big Ben strikes five o'clock in the afternoon. Sounds of* **Emily***, who has fallen asleep. She begins to murmur and fret and this gradually grows in intensity to full-blown nightmare. A jangling of keys offstage. A dim light illuminates the chapel undercroft from the outer area of St Stephen's Hall. Sound of footsteps slowly descending stairs*]

Enter **Mary**

[*The dark figure of a woman, moving slowly and deliberately across the stage. The figure, now distinguishable as* **Mary** *flops into a wooden upright chair for a breather. It is now the morning of Saturday 1st April*]

Mary Can't see a bleedin' thing in 'ere!

[*Exit* **Mary***, going off to turn the light on at the bottom of the stairs*

[*Lighting change*

Enter **Mary**

[*Wearily, she sits back down on the chair, rubs her aching foot and groans.* **Mary** *hears a similar murmur from behind which startles her but dismisses this as her imagination. She decides to move to the cupboard to find what she came for*]

Mary Come on Mary, no such thing as ghosts! [*Not quite believing it*] Not even the ghost of Guy Fawkes. Brasso! [*She approaches the cupboard*]

Emily [*shouting*] Nooooooo!

Mary Oooohh!

Emily [*shouting*] Leave me alone!

Mary [*taking fright, calling*] Mr Bennett!!

Emily [*shouting*] I shall be sick!!

Mary [*returning cautiously*] What's that? Who's in there?

[*Silence*]

Mary [*cautiously*] Is anyone in there??

[*Sound of someone kicking a metal pail. Taking courage,* **Mary** *picks up a mop and braces herself*]

Mary Come out and show yourself!

[*Silence*]

Mary Right. [**Mary** *steels herself and marches towards the cupboard door, tries the handle, the door doesn't budge*] What?! What on earth? Open this door! [**Mary** *pushes as hard as she can and the door opens an inch, but is very abruptly pushed back*] Flamin' 'eck! [*Pause*] Who's in there? [*Silence*] Who are you? Open this door! [*She pushes the door again*] Right then, I'm off to report this . . .

Emily [*with great intensity*] Beloved Saint Joan. Protect me.

Mary Who? Joan – who?

Emily I am Saint Joan!

Mary What's going on?

Emily I'm fighting for justice.

Mary Flamin' 'eck!

Emily Justice! For me, for you, for all women!

Mary How on earth did you get in 'ere?

Emily It wasn't difficult.

Mary Are you one of them, a suffragette?

Emily I am Saint Joan!

Mary Saint Joan? Not Queen Victoria then?

Emily Of course not!

Mary Oh . . . you've come from Bedlam have you? The 'ospital, have you?

Emily No, I haven't!

Mary You're Joan, are you?

Emily Joan is a woman in a man's world. She is my eternal inspiration.

Mary Oh, I see. Well dear, you won't find no inspiration in there, will you? I'll just go and fetch Mr Bennett, he'll be able to help you . . .

Emily *Please, please.* I must remain undiscovered until Monday morning.

Mary Monday! Why??

Emily You must know what's happening on Sunday night.

Mary Sunday? [*Penny drops*] Oh! You're one of *them,* are you? Suffragette. Well I dunno what your game is, but I know what's happening *Saturday* night – tonight – and I need to get in this cupboard! Brasso, silver polish. [*Walking off*] I'm off to get Mr Bennett!

Emily Wait – please don't go! What's your name?

Mary I'm sorry, Miss. [*Leaving*]

Emily I'll do . . . anything.

Mary [**Emily's** *tone causes* **Mary** *to stop dead*] What? To stay in this cupboard? What for?

Emily [*pause*] What's your name?

Mary My *name??* [*Softening*] My name's Mary Tatton.

Emily Mary.

Mary Mary, Miss.

Emily Mary?

Mary Yes, Miss?

Emily Do you really *have* to get into this cupboard?

Mary Yes, I do Miss! It's my master's birthday today and we've got his party to prepare for.

Emily But Sunday night . . .

Mary We're out of brass and silver polish and I've been told there's some in here. All the doorplates need doing and all the silverware! I gotta get in there! Open this door! [*Pushes door*]

Emily Do you know what Sunday night is?

Mary 'course I do. It's Census Night, but my master takes care of all that. Nothing to do with me, I don't count. Look Miss, I gotta get this stuff, I gotta lot to do!

Emily Your master?

Mary Mr Lowther.

Emily Mr Lowther?

Mary Mr Lowther, Speaker of the House of Commons. In case you didn't know.

Emily As it happens, I do know. I'm also aware of Mr Lowther's views on women's suffrage.

Mary Well, Miss . . .

Emily Sunday is Census Night. Thousands of us women are uniting in our refusal to submit to this. We'll be hiding in darkened houses, barricading the doors, defacing our Census forms . . .

Mary But why, Miss? It's just a few names on a page. Mr Lowther thinks it's a good thing, he says it'll be an 'elp. What harm can it do?

Emily *Harm?* Women must be included in the shaping of our future. Yes, this Census is intended to provide information so that the Government can improve the living conditions of ordinary working people. But, Mary who knows *more* about the difficulties of domestic affairs than women – disease, hunger, destitution – and who knows *less* about their hardships than those gentlemen sitting in Parliament? *That's* the harm, that's the hypocrisy! Why should the millions of women in this land comply with the Government's request for information when they allow us no voice or means to express our views? We are invisible, we do not count, therefore we shall not be counted.

[*Sound of footsteps above. The women freeze*]

Emily What's that?

Mary Ssh!

[*They hear the undercroft door creaking open*]

Emily [*whispering*] Please . . .

Mary [*shouting up the stairs*] Morning, Mr Bennett, it's all right, it's just me, Mary, from Speaker's House. Just fetchin' some Brasso and silver polish. [*Pause*]

Mr Bennett [*offstage*] Very well, just don't forget the key.

Mary Right you are Mr Bennett, I'll return the key to the Sergeant's office.

[*Sound of door closing and* **Mr Bennett** *walking away*]

Emily [*pause*] Thank you.

Mary S'cuse me Miss, but couldn't you find a more convenient place to hide?

Emily Oh, this is only the first part of my mission, *I have a greater purpose* ——

Mary What's that then?

Emily On Monday morning a woman's voice will be heard, it will be heard in the Ho ——

Mary Right miss. I need my stuff. I've got me work to do and they'll be wondering where I am. If I'm here much longer, I'll be in trouble. Look, in that cupboard, on your right, not on the shelf, but on the floor beneath it – there's a box of polishes . . . now . . .

Emily Can I trust you?

Mary Trust! I've had enough of this [*marching to the door, shouting*] Give me my polish! [*Realising she's being too loud, quieter*] Give me my polish!

[*In the meantime, **Emily** has moved the boxes and has the box of polishes in her hand. **Mary** walks away from the door in order to take a running shove. As **Mary** turns, the door suddenly opens six inches and **Emily** thrusts out the box of polish*]

Mary Oh [*slightly put out*] much obliged. [**Mary** *makes to leave, but lingers*] Look Miss, what you're doing is your business and I want no part of it. But, if you want to change your mind, you could leave with me, now? The tours will be starting soon, but I reckon I can get you out now, while it's quiet.

Emily No thank you, Mary. [*Beat*] It's necessary that I stay.

Mary You said Monday?

Emily 'til Monday.

Mary [*walks off into the cloakroom and returns with a cup of water*] Look Miss, Monday morning's a long way off. There's a cloakroom through there. Here's some water, if you're thirsty. [*Places mug on the chair*]

Emily [*pause*] Mary, will you keep this a secret? [*Beat*] Do I have your word?

Mary No, I can't give you my word – bloody hell! S'cuse me, Miss. [*Pause*] Well Miss, I haven't seen yer, have I? I dunno you're 'ere. Could be the ghost of Guy Fawkes . . . [*Walks up the steps*]

[*Exit **Mary**, locking the door*

[**Emily** *listens and waits a beat to make sure* **Mary** *has gone. Then she opens the door, races out of the cupboard, grabs the mug and quickly consumes the water*]

[*Blackout*

Scene Two

Sunday morning – 2nd April

Music: part of the final verse of The March of the Women
[distant and ethereal] begins

Light from the stained-glass window gradually fades up on
Emily, *kneeling on a prayer stool downstage. She sees in her
prayer her vision of St. Joan. She seems to be having a restorative
experience of some kind.*

Enter **Mary**, *halfway through the song*

[Holding the polish box **Mary** *stands watching* **Emily**]

Emily (*singing*) *Life, strife – these two are one,*
Naught can ye win but by faith and daring;
On, on, that ye have done
But for the work of today preparing.

[Towards the end of the song, **Mary** *retreats]*

[Exit **Mary**

[**Emily** *stands up and stretches]*

Emily Thoughts have gone forth whose powers can sleep
no more!

[**Mary** *can be heard making her presence felt offstage]*

Enter **Mary**

[**Mary** *is carrying the box of polishes. She stands a moment*]

Mary Are you here, Miss?

[*Silence.* **Mary** *cautiously goes to the cupboard and taps on the door*]

Mary Miss? It's Mary.

Emily From Speaker's House?

Mary Yes.

Emily What day is it?

Mary It's Sunday morning – early, Miss.

Emily Census Night, tonight.

Mary Yes, Miss.

Emily One more day, one more night . . .

Mary Then you can go home.

Emily I doubt if I shall be going home.

Mary Why's that, Miss?

Emily Because on Monday morning I will be in the House of Commons.

Mary You can't do that, Miss.

Emily I can.

Mary No, you can't

Emily Yes, I can.

Mary They closed the Ladies' Gallery after that Australian actress chained herself to the grille, and they took hours to free her from it. Special entry only now. She's spoilt it for the lot of you. Went to Holloway Prison for a month she did.

Emily I intend to enter the House itself.

Mary You can't.

Emily I can. I can and I will.

Mary Don't even try those tricks in the House of Commons, Miss. Is there nothin' sacred to you? It's Parliament! I know what you lot have done to St Stephen's Hall, up there [*gesturing, angrily*]. Painting all over the walls, breaking bits off the statues. That's not right. And you know what they do to your women in the streets – man-handled, thrown to the ground, beaten – by the crowds, by the police. You don't want to be treated like that, Miss . . .

Emily I've known worse.

Mary What worse, Miss?

Emily In prison.

Mary [*shocked*] You've been to prison, Miss?

Emily Yes; I consider it an honour.

Mary An honour – it's a disgrace!

Emily I consider it the greatest honour to fight for women's freedom. What nobler cause could there be?

Mary What did they put you in for?

Emily Obstruction, stone throwing, smashing windows.

Mary Well, I think you suffragettes should stop throwing your weight about. Throwing stones, smashing people's windows, shouting in the street! You're a bloody nuisance. S'cuse me Miss. Have you any idea how many men it took to free that woman from the grille? Six! Tell me this, when you're doing your smashing, do you ever think about the poor sod who's gotta clear it up? And who's paying for it – not you lot! You should be ashamed!

Emily I am *not* ashamed. I have already paid for it by sacrificing friends, family, my health – you have no idea the brutality we receive in prison – my good name. *My good name.* In this humiliation, I suffer most.

Mary What happened in prison then?

Emily I can't . . . speak about that.

[*Pause.* **Emily** *clearly upset and* **Mary** *doesn't know what to say, but listens*]

Emily [*after a long pause*] You think I'm mad, don't you? You think, why would any woman in their right mind behave in this way and how dare someone of my privilege go on about suffering when many would argue I have never really known it? And you would be right, in part; I have money or the means to make it and I have always had a roof over my head, enough food to eat and never gone barefoot. But what you also need to understand is that I'm fighting for all women to have a voice, for me and for you, Mary. The moment is now, Mary. This Census is supposed to help bring about change for those in need, but . . .

Mary That's just what Mr Lowther said . . .

Emily Women *need* the vote. You can tell them what's needed, Mary to make things better. You know more than they do, you do count. Your vote could be very important, more than that – vital, necessary. For you, for me, for our children, for our children's children . . .

Mary My dad worked down the docks. My family were poor, very poor. I had eight brothers and sisters, but three of them died. Diphtheria, typhoid. In the winter, we was sent out to beg for coal. Living was hard. I didn't want to leave home, but it was one less mouth for my mum and dad to feed. Coming into service has been a better life for me.

Emily My life – was different – I was comfortable. I worked as a governess. A good family, beautiful surroundings, but I longed to get back to London, the centre of the universe.

Mary Yes Miss, I know what you mean, the centre of the universe.

Emily In the beginning I was intrigued by – although somewhat disapproving of – the suffragette movement. I was curious about the WSPU meetings. The photographs in the newspapers showed such a brightness in the eyes of the campaigners. They were alive! They weren't living a humdrum existence, trapped by their employment or position. And the articles that followed these pictures, the unfavourable claims and assertions made about these women – couldn't possibly be right. I had to see for myself. I chose my first meeting with none other than Mrs Pankhurst herself to speak.

Mary [*impressed*] Mrs Pankhurst . . .

Emily There was a hush in the hall as she swept on to the stage. The group of young girls in front were almost swooning. This was not for a matinee idol, not for a man. [*Laughs*] Mrs Pankhurst is charming, handsome – yes, but she's a *woman*. A married, middle-aged woman!

Mary [*laughing*] Well I never!

Emily And then she spoke: 'We are here, not because we are law-breakers; we are here in our efforts to become law-makers.' Silence. You could hear a pin drop. Then the room shook with applause.

Mary So what did you do then?

Emily I joined them. There and then.

Mary And these other refined ladies, do they think it's right to break the law?

Emily We don't want to break the law. For years we have campaigned peacefully and we've got nowhere, we've been ignored. We are fighting for a better future for all. We break the law as a last resort, it is the only way, it's necessary. There will come a time when women will no longer be constrained, no longer cabined and confined!

Mary Well you can always open the door, Miss. What does Mrs Pankhurst think about you doing this, shutting yourself in cupboards?

Emily Actually, she doesn't know I'm here. I act alone.

Mary Well, you're a very naughty girl – how can bring yourself to behave like this?

Emily When I break the law it's not *me*. One has to step outside oneself, do you see? When I go home my mother always says: 'Emily, what have you been doing? I have seen such and such a thing in the paper and I know you were in it.' I reply: 'But how can you? When I am going to do anything, I always put you quite away from me, quite out of my mind.' I call it being under the influence. Steel yourself and then you can do anything.

Mary Your mother's your mother! You might put thoughts of her out your mind, but that don't stop her wondering and worrying about you. You're deliberately putting yourself in harm's way.

Emily Yes I am and there is a heavy price to pay for breaking the law – when you walk through the gates of a prison; you die!

Mary You *die?*

Emily You cease to be a person. No one talks to you, except to issue an order and you must not speak to another soul.

Mary Not speak?

Emily You'd be amazed what you try and read into a snatched glance from an inmate; what comfort there is from a few words scratched on a cell wall. When you come out, back into the real world, nothing appears to have changed – the people go about just the same, the buses buzz along the streets, but you know things have changed forever. You hear questions, you hear yourself respond, but you're hovering outside yourself; you're dead.

Mary You really want to do these things?

Emily This is my mission. I dedicate my life to it. I have no choice in this matter.

Mary Miss Emily . . . you were praying earlier . . .

Emily To St. Joan. [*Beat*] She talks to me.

Mary What does she say?

Emily She gives me strength, she gives me hope, she sustains me.

Mary I think you need something to eat, Miss.

Emily I'll not be fed again . . . [*crash from the cupboard as* **Emily** *faints and falls off the boxes*]

Mary Miss??

[**Mary** *rushes to the cupboard and tries to push the door open, but* **Emily**'s *weight against the door prevents this*]

Mary Are you all right? [*Shouting*] Emily!

Emily [*murmuring incoherently*] Not by the *junior* doctor . . .

Mary You're up against the door – I can't move it! [*Noises of agony from the cupboard*] Oh Lord!! Help – Mr Ben—!! [*Rushes to get more water*] More water here, Miss! Don't worry, I'll be back soon!

[**Mary** *rushes up the stairs as Big Ben chimes eight o'clock in the morning*]

[*Exit* **Mary**

[*Lights fade*

Scene Three

Sunday morning – 2nd April – about eleven o'clock

Enter **Emily**

[*She wanders on from the side with some water, a pencil and notebook. She is composing the speech she intends to make in the House of Commons on Monday morning*]

Emily Gentlemen of the House of Commons, I address you on behalf of all the women of England . . . no [*crossing out vigorously*] I ask you – no, too weak! I implore you? Women of England demand [*discovers the light of St. Joan and this provides the sudden inspiration*] Do *justice* to the women of England by passing the Women's Enfranchisement Bill in 1911! [**Emily** *raises her cup to St. Joan*] Thank you! [*Takes a sip of water and then lowers the cup and prays*] St. Joan – my refuge and strength, a very present help in trouble. Therefore, I will not fear though the earth be removed and the mountains be carried into the midst of the sea!

[**Emily** *hears the jangling of keys, re-enters the cupboard, closes the door, perches on boxes with her foot up against the door frame*]

Enter **Mary** approaching the cupboard cautiously

Mary [*quietly*] Miss? Miss Emily? Are you there, Miss Emily?

Emily Mary ——?

Mary Thank the Lord, Miss – are you all right? I think you fainted. I left some water by the door, here – did you find it?

Emily Yes, thank you, Mary. It was a great help.

Mary It's me day off today. I just came over earlier to return these bits, but you weren't well so I come back – brought you something to eat.

Emily What is it, Mary?

Mary Something sweet – give me your hand, give me your hand! [**Emily** *slowly opens a crack in the door and puts her hand out*] A treat. [**Mary** *puts a piece of wrapped cake in* **Emily**'s *hand*]

Emily Oh – cake!

Mary Mr Lowther's birthday cake – we've all had a piece.

Emily Oh Mary – thank you! [*Eats a mouthful*] It's delicious, will you share it with me?

Mary It's for you, Miss.

Emily Let's share it [*handing some back*].

Mary Oh – much obliged, I'm sure, Miss! [*Sitting down on the prayer stool*]

[*They eat.* **Emily** *coughs*]

Mary You can taste the brandy, can't you?

Emily [*laughing*] Eating his cake now . . . Mr Lowther doesn't like me very much!

Mary How do you mean, Miss?

Emily Have you heard of the Index Expurgatorius?

Mary Index Expurger – bloody hell! Sorry Miss. No, I ain't – what is it?

Emily It's a list of undesirable nuisances who are not welcome here. Mr Lowther decides who they are.

Mary I see . . .

[*Silence as they eat*]

Mary They give you cake in prison?

Emily [*she suddenly stops eating, wraps up the cake*] No, nothing like that.

Mary Well, what did they give you then?

Emily It's WSPU policy to refuse food as soon as you go in.

Mary So they gave it to you, but you wouldn't eat it?

[*Silence*]

Emily If you don't eat it, they force it on you.

Mary They force it on you?

Emily They won't recognise us as political prisoners . . .

Mary You've gotta eat, you'll starve.

Emily It's the most powerful tool, the only one we have in there . . .

Mary Why don't you just close your mouth?

Emily Mary – there's so much you don't know. They find a way. [*Pause*] Half a dozen wardresses come into your cell with the doctors. 'I am going to feed you by force.' They hold you down so you can't move. They lie you flat or tie you to a chair. If you don't open your mouth, the doctor (a junior one if you're unlucky), forces it with a steel gag and screws it wide open. The doctor tried all round my mouth with a steel gag to find an opening. On the right side of my mouth there two teeth are missing, here. He found this gap, pushed in the gag, prised open my mouth to its widest extent, then forced two feet of rubber tube down my throat. At the top of the tube is a funnel. A wardress poured liquid down my throat out of a tin enameled cup.

[*Mary looks at the tin enameled water cup that has been left on the chair*]

Mary That must be terrible . . . what's in the cup?

Emily Raw eggs, milk and some foul medicament. [*Slight pause,* **Mary** *wraps the last of her cake up, no longer hungry for it*] It was a horror. The memory of it will haunt me for the rest of my life.

[*Sound of footsteps approaching quickly from above*]

Mary I left the keys outside in the lock!! [**Mary** *dashes to retrieve them, but only gets to the bottom of the stairs*]

Constable 'ello? Keys in the lock?

[**Mary** *rushes back.* **Emily** *opens the cupboard door and reaches her hand out to* **Mary** *who scrambles inside.* **Mary** *squeezes past to hide behind* **Emily** *who shuts the cupboard door. The undercroft door creaks open*]

Constable [*offstage*] 'ello – anybody there? No. Someone's for it. [*Shouting*] It's all right Mr Bennett, no one here. [*Sound of keys turning in the lock*] Reckon it's time for my cuppa . . .

[*They listen as the* **Constable** *walks away*]

Mary [*in the darkness of the cupboard*] Locked it! He's locked it! I'm shut in! Oh Lord – what have I done. I'll be in so much trouble.

Emily Mary, Mary – you've done nothing.

Mary I can't stay here, Miss. I work for Mr Lowther. [*Pushes past* **Emily** *and out of the cupboard back into the undercroft*] It's Census Night, I gotta be back by six! [*Shouting*] Help!

[**Emily** *rushes out of the cupboard and attempts to calm* **Mary** *down*]

Emily Mary, Mary . . . it'll be all right! We'll find a way – let's think . . .

Mary I'm done for . . .

Emily No, let's think . . . you got locked in by mistake; you were in the cloakroom and didn't hear the man call . . .

Mary Supposed to be at my sister's . . .

Emily You called after him, ran up the stairs, but he'd gone . . .

Mary I was taken ill and I missed the omnibus . . .

Emily You fainted down here and bumped your head . . .

Mary Her little girl was taken ill and I had to stay with her while me sister went off to fetch the doctor . . .

Emily I locked you in and held you hostage . . .

Mary I could . . . [**Mary** *looks at* **Emily** *properly for the first time, the penny drops*] . . . red hair . . .

Emily Yes . . .

Mary You're the redhead.

Emily What do you mean?

Mary I've seen you before.

Emily Possibly, I'm here quite a lot.

Mary I know who you are . . . you're on that list . . . Oh my Lord! You're an . . . undesirable!

[*Lights fade as Big Ben ticks on . . .*

Scene Four

A few hours have passed. It is now four o'clock on Sunday afternoon. Lights up on **Emily** *seated on prayer stool with her carpet bag next to her. The notes for* **Emily**'s *speech are all over the floor.*

Mary *comes slowly across the undercroft floor from the door*

Emily How many times have you tried that door now, Mary?

Mary Well, if someone should happen to unlock it, it'd be better for the both of us.

[**Mary** *doesn't sit down, but continues to pace the floor, anxiously. Big Ben chimes four o'clock. The women count the chimes to determine the time of day*]

Mary [*to herself*] Could say the omnibus broke down or me sister was taken ill . . . so I got 'numerated there...?

Emily My plan remains unaltered, Mary.

Mary Oh yes, the speech in the Commons. Still on that, Miss?

Emily Still on that. It's nearly finished, but not quite. It needs more punch, I need to make it personal.

Mary Even, if by some miracle you manage to get in there, Miss, four policemen will seize you and cart you out before you can open your mouth.

Emily Not if I'm attached to the chamber itself! [**Emily** *raises a lock and chain from her open carpet bag*]

Mary Oh Lord!

[**Emily** *laughs*]

Mary [*angrily*] This is just a big joke to you, is it? Do you think for a minute about the lives you're wreckin'? There'll be questions asked of us when they find you, jobs on the line. Families wrecked! Is that personal enough for you, Miss?

Emily Mary ——

Mary I will lose my job, after forty-three years of service. I will lose my job because I helped yer, because I felt sorry for yer, because I was worried [*breaking*] that you'd die, on your own in this undercroft.

Emily Mary, you must know how grateful ——

Mary I don't want your thanks – what use is that to me? All right, Mr Lowther doesn't want the likes of you 'ere and you don't like Mr Lowther or what Mr Lowther thinks. So, it's fun for you to play tricks and hide in cupboards to make your point. To me, Mr Lowther is . . . family. I've worked for the family since I was a girl of fourteen, when this Speaker Lowther was still at Eton. I'm fifty-eight years old now, so it's been a long time. I've never worked for anyone else, and I'm sure I wouldn't know how to now... [**Mary** *sinks down into the chair*]

Emily That is a long time.

Mary It's a life time. [*After a pause*] What I do is light the fires in the morning and do any cleaning I'm asked. It's a very busy day, 'specially in the winter. I'm a Necessary Woman, Miss, and I am necessary that's for sure. I'm the one that does the fires. No one knows how to light a fire better than I do. Master always says: 'I need to be warm Mary, I cannot work, I cannot think straight, unless I'm warm!' I got my own special way to twist and loop the paper, so it's right. It's my special way, old newspaper, that's what I use. Can't use too much though, otherwise you'd smother the flame, you got to build in the kindling. Just small little sticks of wood, so you've got a pile, like a little mountain, built so the air can get through. Because that's what a fire needs – air. Then, you can put a match to it and when that little mountain of kindle gets going and it's flaming away, then you build your coal into it – see my hands, Miss? That's because of the coal, it don't go away now, even when I scrub them, that's coal dust that is – but now you got to watch it, you got to watch it! You turn around at all or just take your eyes off it, and it'll go out. It'll escape you, it's gone! And then you'll have to start again. Keep your eyes on it, and then when the coal catches proper you can add more, and then perhaps more. That's called banking it up. So, then it lasts and the room's getting warmer and warmer. It's magic really, how it all changes, and that's because of me, I know how.

Emily You're a valuable woman, Mary.

Mary Well I suppose I am, Miss Emily, in that! [*Pause*] I'm a necessary woman. I get up at half past four every morning to light those flaming fires... all day long I'm tending them, keeping them *alive*!

Emily You've been very loyal to the Lowthers.

Mary Well I have Miss. And they've been very good to me. [*Pause*] You see, Miss, years ago – I worked for old Mr Lowther, then. I hadn't been working for them that long really – I got into a bit of trouble, I was young and foolish Miss, and so ashamed, and I was desperate. At first, it weren't noticeable so I could keep it quiet, but I knew that wouldn't last. I'd have to say something. In the end I told the Housekeeper how it was and she took me straight to the Mistress. It were terrible, I could hardly bring myself to speak about it.

Emily What happened then?

Mary Well, the Mistress was very kind. She found somewhere for me to be while I had the baby. But she had to speak to Mr Lowther of course. I thought I'd never see them again, but after it was all over they had me back. They had me back! So I started working for them again, and I was so grateful. It was as though nothing had ever happened.

Emily And your . . . *baby?*

Mary I wasn't supposed to know, but one of the nurses told me it was a girl. A little girl. I was told she'd be up for adoption. Up for adoption. So, she's around somewhere. And living a better life than I could have given her I'm sure. I called her Daisy but no one knew that. My Daisy. But of course, that's not her name now.

Emily She would be about my age?

Mary She would.

Emily She could be a suffragette!

Mary Well, Miss Emily, I never thought of that. [*Pause*] She wouldn't dare!

[**Emily** *starts to pick up her scattered speech papers from the floor*]

Mary Look Miss, I know what you're doing is important to you, but they've been good to me, the Lowthers and now I've let them down again.

Emily You were only doing what you thought was right.

Mary But when they find out, find us here – together, they won't see things that way. I should've reported it, from the word go, sorry Miss.

Emily I'm so glad you didn't.

Mary You want to get caught tomorrow though, don't you? I just want to keep my job. I still might if I could just get out of here – no one will have missed me yet, 'cept me sister, I was supposed to see her today.

Emily When will they be raising the alarm – after six?

Mary The 'numerator's coming to call. Mr Lowther made such a big thing about it, gave all the staff a lecture on the importance of the Census, before his party last night. A five pound fine, they're saying if you miss it. Five pounds! Wherever will I find that? Mr Lowther was very serious . . .

Emily Was he?

Mary He was, but he was in a joking – how do you say it?

Emily Jocular?

Mary Jocular mood.

Emily I suppose it was his birthday . . .

[*They look at each other and smile*]

Emily You said you know me?

Mary I've seen you before. I recognise the red hair, now you're out of your hiding place. I saw you last year. You were being led out by a couple of policemen, across Old Palace Yard. You looked . . . you were covered in dust and dirt!

Emily I'd been hiding somewhere else that day – in a ventilation shaft.

Mary A ventilation shaft? Where –? How on earth did you get in there?

Emily Luck really. I was on the end of a tour moving through the Great Central Hall. There was a little passage beyond it, tried a door which was unlocked. There was a policeman, but at that moment he was looking the wrong way, so I slipped in. In the wall of the corridor beyond, there was a little glass window that led to the ventilation shaft. I crawled in.

Mary And no one found you?

Emily No – there was a series of ladders going higher into the tower. I reached the first platform with difficultly and perched there. It was very uncomfortable and dangerous. I was terrified of falling off.

Mary Flamin' 'eck!

Emily I hid there for almost twenty-eight hours. Was very dirty and dusty and the pipes made it terribly hot.

Mary You looked like a little chimney sweep, when I saw you. Thought a bit of luck might be coming my way . . .

Emily I was slightly better prepared in that I had some food – chocolate and bananas – but I couldn't last because I desperately needed water.

Mary 'course you needed water!

Emily I came out of the shaft and found a little tap right there in the wall.

Mary Oh my Lord, thank goodness!

Emily The sign next to the tap said 'Cold'.

Mary Oh Miss . . .

Emily Water's never tasted so good! After that I could have waited in that shaft for days . . . dozing off, listening out for the chimes of Big Ben and the afternoon bells of the Abbey, footsteps . . .

Mary Miss – you could've died.

Emily Could have been locked in, could have died of thirst, fallen off the platform . . .

[**Mary** *looks at* **Emily**. **Mary** *is silent*]

Emily In the end, it was the *water* that gave me away.

Mary How's that, Miss?

Emily Constable came past on his rounds and must have seen the water on the floor. All of a sudden the door opened and he looked in. I must have looked ghastly covered in grime, a terrible apparition! He was trembling so much he nearly dropped his lantern. He shouted 'What is it?', banged the door back and blew his whistle. Another constable came and they carted me off to be washed . . .

Mary That must have been when I saw yer. You were such a sight – I remember! Is that when they put you on the blacklist?

Emily Soon after that. I broke some windows in the Crown Office . . .

Mary 'Silly woman!' That's what Mr Lowther said. I heard him talking about it to the Serjeant-at-Arms: 'What did she hope to achieve?' 'Nothing, but making herself uncomfortable and look ridiculous...'

Emily Well, I certainly looked ridiculous.

Mary Yes Miss.

Emily [*looking at* **Mary**] Not as if they have never seen a woman covered in dust before . . .

Mary No Miss . . . [*Pause*] On your own, in the dark all the time, no one to help yer. You gotta lot of pluck, Miss. I don't know how you keep going.

Emily I keep going because . . . I have to. I've told you before, it's not a matter of choice. I am inspired by the shining light of St. Joan. Hers was a life of action in which she broke all the rules. I *will* follow this path to wherever it takes me. Through my humble work in this noblest of all causes, I have become fulfilled. I am blessed! I have an interest in living which I've never experienced before. What would I do now, anyway, if I wasn't a suffragette? I dare say I could work as a governess again; no.

Mary So, you sacrificed everything for your cause. You must have great faith that you'll win; you've given up your life to fight for it.

Emily I have faith in my mission. Courage, persistence, determination. Persistence – that's the key.

Mary Headstrong, wilful, rebellious, naughty – that's been your key!

[***Emily*** *laughs heartily*]

Mary [*remembering*] Key . . . spare key . . . spare key . . .

Emily [*jumping up after* **Mary**] Spare key – is there one? Do you know that?

Mary Sometimes there's all night vigils down 'ere. That's why they have the cloakroom. One of the Members got locked in one night by mistake so after that they had to leave a spare key . . .

[*They frantically search for a spare key.* **Mary** *rushes out into the corridor,* **Emily** *rushes into the cupboard. Both find nothing. Moment of realisation – they rush into the cloakroom*]

[*Exit* **Emily** *and* **Mary**

Mary [*offstage*] Well I'll be!

Enter **Emily**, *holding the key aloft, followed by* **Mary**

Mary Try it Miss! Try it in the door . . .

[*Exit* **Emily**, *going upstairs to try the key*

[*The key can be heard turning in the lock*]

Enter **Emily**

Emily Door's open – quick, quick!

[**Mary** *starts to leave, but stops to thank St. Joan*]

Mary [*curtsies to St. Joan*] Thank you!!

Emily Quickly!

Mary Thank you, Miss.

Emily Thank you, Mary. You've made *this* stay in Parliament more than bearable.

[*They embrace*]

Emily Go forth and be enumerated!!

[*Exit* **Mary**

[**Emily** *locks the door behind her*]

Enter **Emily**, *holding the key*

[*She is about to put the key in her pocket, but then decides to put it back in the cloakroom*]

[*Exit* **Emily**

Enter **Emily**

[*She purposefully picks up her bag.* **Emily** *dresses in the blackout*]

Scene Five

Early Monday morning – 3rd April – sounds of bells pealing.
Emily *is putting her gloves on in the cupboard, gathering her things and making her final preparations. She hears* **Mary**'s *knocking and then her urgent low whisper.*

Mary [*offstage*] Miss, Miss! Are you there, Miss? Let me in!

> [*Exit* **Emily**, *moving swiftly to collect the key from the cloakroom*

> *Enter* **Emily**, *with the key*

> [*Exit* **Emily**, *disappearing up the stairs*

Enter **Mary**, *after a moment, rushing in, followed by* **Emily**

Emily What's happened, why are you here again?

Mary Census Night! It's all over the papers!

Emily What do the papers say? Was the boycott a success?

Mary I don't know, Miss, I've no idea, but they reckon there's going to be trouble on College Green this morning. The Serjeant-at-Arms is bringing in special constables in to guard St Stephen's Hall, be all over the place in half an hour. Come with me now Miss and I can get you out!

Emily Mary ——

Mary I can't stay long, Miss. Please, come with me now!

Emily Is the Commons open yet?

Mary I don't know, Miss – Mr Lowther leaves the house at nine o'clock.

Emily Do you think it'll be open for cleaning?

Mary Cleaning?? Listen to me, Emily. You're a brave young woman, but this is foolish. We women need you to speak up for us and continue the fight with your words. How can you do that if you're shut up in jail. It's not good for you Miss, it's not good for us.

Emily I have the words. I just need to be in the Commons to be heard!

[*Sound of constables gathering outside the building, receiving orders*]

Mary They're comin' into St Stephen's Hall, they'll be searching all round here. Come on Miss!

Emily Help me get into the House of Commons!

Mary I ——

[**Mary** *is about to answer when there are sounds of boots in St Stephen's Hall above*]

Mary Too late, Miss. [*With purpose*] Have you got your speech?

Emily Yes: here [*points to her bag*] and *here* [*points to head*]

Mary Ready?

Emily Ready.

[**Mary** *picks up a wooden box that says* Pears Soap *on the side*]

Mary Then do it for me, now. [**Mary** *places box DSC, collects hat from chair*] Do it for Daisy [**Mary** *hands* **Emily** *her hat which she puts on and helps* **Emily** *onto the box*] Do it for us.

[**Mary** *moves into audience or to the side of the stage and listens*]

Emily Gentlemen of the House of Commons, do justice
to the women of England by passing the Women's
Enfranchisement Bill in 1911. The women of Australia
were given the vote in King Edward's coronation year;
give the women of England a similar right on the
coronation of King George and Queen Mary. Queen
Mary is British born, and if votes were given to women
in the year of her coronation they would bear a special
mark of appreciation.

For too long British women have been overlooked and
ignored, their vital contribution to society disregarded.

We are denied the basic right to choose, have a say, to take
part in the shaping of our Country. Why is it that half the
population of this land is ignored?

Women are the core – we are *required* – the life-blood
of this nation – without us there will be no future. We
are mothers, we raise our families, go out to work,
pay our taxes, carry out our civic duties in good faith.
University graduates, teachers, doctors, lawyers, servants,
mill-workers, cleaners – in all walks of life women are
there – necessary and indispensable.

There are women working under this very roof, in
Parliament, who are unheard and unseen – invisible –
ghost women! You will not have noticed them, but they
are there in the shadows – the Angels of the House.
These women prepare your meals, wash your floors,
build your fires to keep you warm. These women are
enablers, they make the work of government possible.

Why should their sacrifice be ignored, why should *we* be
denied a voice? Gentlemen of the House, a new dawn is
breaking! For this generation and generations to come.

Do justice to the women of England! The answer lies in
  your hands . . .

[*Noises from St Stephen's Hall above and from outside the
undercroft. The door is unlocked*]

Constable [*offstage, shouting*] Who's down there?

Emily [*shouting*] My name is Emily Wilding Davison.
  [*Police whistle sounds, clatter of boots down the steps*] I am a
  suffragette [*faces front*] and it is my *ambition* to enter the
  House!

[*Blackout*

[The March of the Women *plays*